GLOSSARY
of
BITCOIN
TERMS
and
DEFINITIONS

J. Anthony Malone

ISBN: 978-1-312-98415-8

NoHoMedia
North Hollywood CA 91601

818-508-4408
Twitter: @a5ym4e

Some unusual terms are frequently used in Bitcoin documentation and discussions of virtual currencies which now deserve some explanation.

This Glossary is intended to help the reader understand the meaning of Bitcoin related terms.

21 Million

The total number of bitcoins that will be issued will be 21 million. This number has been programmed into the protocol and can never be changed. Whether by accident or design, the present Bitcoin system defines a currency with extreme deflationary characteristics.

6 Confirmations

Each Bitcoin transaction is broadcast to all **nodes**, or computers, using the Bitcoin client. When the miners confirm a block, a page in the Bitcoin ledger is published attesting that the transactions in that block are valid and that no attempt has been made to spend those bitcoins on two or more things at the same time. This protocol is known as a "confirmation" and occurs every ten minutes, on average.

Transactions become effective after they have been referenced in a **block**, which serve as the official record of executed transactions. Transactions may only be listed in a block if they satisfy such conditions as valid timestamping and absence of double spending.

One confirmation is considered secure. Having 6 confirmations is considered proof that there is statistically no chance that any cheating has occurred.

51% Attack

The Bitcoin network is essentially a democracy with each miner having having one vote. The system is secure if at least 51% of the participants abide by the protocol. If more than 51% of the mining power is concentrated in one miner or group of miners, they could invalidate transactions, create false transactions and change the Bitcoin protocol.

As a result of the rise in mining pools where persons with a small amount of computing power join a pool and receive payment on the percentage of their contribution, the risk of one group assembling 51% or more control is real but may be tempered by the fact that in this event the integrity in the Bitcoin system and the value of the currency would be compromised, to the financial detriment of the majority miners.

In early 2014, as one mining pool came close to surpassing the 50% threshold, it discouraged others from joining the pool to protect the integrity of the system.

Such a "hostile takeover" of Bitcoin is possible in theory. However many experts doubt it is likely.

A **miner** or **mining pool** having majority control with more than 50% of the total computing power devoted to the Bitcoin network could do some damage. The biggest threat is a disruption of the system. However, they could not abscond with currency or hack investors' accounts.

Another real danger, is that centralized control of over 50% of the Bitcoin system would provide a target for government subpoenas and other regulation and control of Bitcoin.

The takeover process would be very expensive. Mining blocks of digital currency requires considerable computing time and energy. In addition, a majority control of the Bitcoin system would have to be sustained for a considerable period of time in order to compromise the system.

Although a potential threat with potentially dramatic results, the Bitcoin protocol was designed with the belief that the work-to-reward ratio would likely deter any attempt to compromise the system in this way.

Address

A Bitcoin address is similar to a physical address or an email address.

An address is a string of letters and numbers. It is the only information needed to send or receive Bitcoin. Each address should only be used in a single transaction. Addresses as safe to share so long as the owner's **private key** is kept secure.

A Bitcoin address is an identifier of 27-34 alphanumeric characters beginning with the number 1 or 3, that represents a destination for a Bitcoin payment. Addresses can be generated at no cost by any user of Bitcoin. At any active Bitcoin site, click "New Address" to be assigned a random address. It is also possible to obtain a Bitcoin address using an account at an exchange or online **wallet service**.

An example of a Bitcoin address: 31uEbMgunupShBVTewXjtqbBv5MndwfXhb.

Bitcoin addresses are really **public keys**. When bitcoins are sent to an address, everyone on the network can see the transfer. However, the holder of the address **private key** (which is stored in their **Wallet**) can actually access the BTC.

A Bitcoin address is a **Base58Check** representation of a **Hash160** of a **public key** with a version byte 0x00 which maps to a prefix "1". Typically represented as text (ex 1CBtcGivXmHQ8ZqdPgeMfcpQNJrqTrSAcG) or as a **QR code**.

A more recent variant of an address is a P2SH address: a **hash** of a spending script with a version byte 0x05 which maps to a prefix "3" (ex 3NukJ6fYZJ5Kk8PjycAnruZkE5Q7UW7i8).

Another variant of an address is not a hash, but a raw private key representation (ex 5KQntKuhYWSRXNqp2yhdXzejkYAR7US3MT1715Mbv5CyUKV 6hVe). This variant is rarely used, limited only to import/export of private keys or printing them on **paper wallets**.

Algorithm

An algorithm is a set of specific instructions that a computer carries out to achieve a desired output.

For Bitcoin the desired outcome is the checksum of a cryptographic block that is submitted back to the Bitcoin Network to confirm transactions.

Altcoin

The collective name for cryptocurrencies offered as alternatives to Bitcoin. A clone of the Bitcoin protocol, with some modifications. (See **Cryptocurrency**)

Bitcoin is the first widely accepted cryptocoin experiment. Others have followed the Bitcoin protocol to develop new cryptocurrency variations, including Litecoin, Primecoin and Ripple, for example.

The modifications are intended to improve or refine the Bitcoin protocol. Litecoin has a quicker transaction confirm time, **scrypt** as **proof-of-work** and higher number of coins. Primecoin finds prime numbers at the same time it confirms its blocks. Namecoin has a special key-value storage.

In theory, an altcoin can be started from an existing Bitcoin blockchain, although no known example exists at this writing. (See also **Fork**.)

At this writing, only Bitcoin has the critical mass to make it a likely success as a cryptocurrency and store of value. The alt-coins are experiments in attributes that could perhaps be adopted by Bitcoin to improve its characteristics and attributes.

Alternative cryptocurrencies using the **SHA-256** hashing algorithm can be mined using the same hardware used to mine Bitcoin such as **FPGA** and **ASIC** devices. **Scrypt** based alt-coins, such as Litecoin, Novacoin and Feathercoin, can be mined using **GPU** cards.

AML

Critics of Bitcoin call for strict regulation of Bitcoin, citing the crypto coin's almost instantaneous transaction time with relative anonymity. Anti-Money Laundering (AML) legislation has been used along with Know Your Client (**KYC**) laws to prosecute some Bitcoin businesses under the guise of money laundering activity.

ASIC

ASIC generally refers to specialized mining chips or entire machines built on these chips. These are the current generation of Bitcoin mining hardware.

Acronym for "application-specific integrated circuit". In other words, a silicon chip specifically designed to perform one specific function and only that function in contrast to **CPU** or **GPU** which perform a wide variety of functions. In the case of Bitcoin, they are designed to process **SHA-256** hashing problems to mine new bitcoins.

ASIC Miner

Computer hardware containing an ASIC chip and configured to mine bitcoins. They can come in the form of boards that plug into a backplane, devices with a USB connector, or standalone devices including all the necessary software, that connect to a network via a wireless link or ethernet cable.

Mining of cryptocurrency data blocks can demand a significant amount of computer space and time, some miners set aside entire machines to do nothing but mining. As the profitability of Bitcoin mining became apparent, miners sought faster and more efficient hardware to maximize profits. These ASIC miners have taken mining out of the hands of the general public and centralized mining in the hands of specialized mining pools.

ASIC devices are custom built powerful machines designed to efficiently hash the cryptography algorithms of the Bitcoin network.

Asymmetric Key Algorithm

The algorithm used to generate public and private keys which are the unique codes essential to cryptocurrency transactions.

If the same password is used to encrypt and decrypt something, this is called a symmetric key algorithm. In that instance both the sender and the receiver have the same key. Each can encrypt and exchange information privately. However since both parties have the decoding information, they cannot keep information private from one another.

With an asymmetric key algorithm, two different passwords are created. Anything encrypted with one can be decrypted by the other. In practice, one is selected to be a *private* key, and kept secret. The other is designated a *public* key and broadcast to the public at large. Both parties have access to the *public* key, but only the person with the *private* key can decode the encryption. This ensures that only that person can access the funds.

Base58

A compact human-readable encoding for binary data invented by Satoshi Nakamoto to make more user-friendly addresses.

This is character coding which reduces the risk of mistaking 1 for I or 0 for O.

Base58Check

A modified Base58 binary-to-text encoding for encoding Bitcoin addresses. It appends the first four bytes of **Hash256** of the encoded data to that data before converting to **Base58**. It is used to detect typing errors in addresses.

BIP

Bitcoin Improvement Protocols. RFC-like documents modeled after PEPs (Python Enhancement Proposals) which discuss different aspects of the protocol and software.

BIPs describe hard fork changes in the core protocol that require supermajority of the Bitcoin community (or, in some cases, only miners) to consent on any change and accept it is an organized manner.

Bitcoin

Bitcoin is a decentralized electronic cash system initially designed and developed by **Satoshi Nakamoto**, whose name is conjectured to be fake by some, and has not been heard from since April 2011.

The design of Bitcoin was first described in a self-published paper, *Bitcoin: a Peer-to-peer electronic cash system*, by Nakamoto in October 2008 after which an open-source project was registered on sourceforge.

The **genesis block** was established on January 3, 2009 and the project was announced on the Cryptography mailing list on January 11, 2009.

Bitcoin uses no complex cryptography. However it is surprisingly ingenious and sophisticated.

Bitcoin has a completely distributed architecture, without any single trusted entity. Bitcoin assumes that the majority of nodes in its network are honest, and resorts to a majority vote mechanism for double spending avoidance and dispute resolution.

The Bitcoin system ensures that users have economic incentives to participate. First, the generation of new bitcoins happens are distributed at a predictable rate. Bitcoin miners solve computational puzzles to generate new bitcoins, while this process is closely aligned with the verification of previous transactions. Miners also collect optional transactional fees for their effort in vetting previous transactions.

Bitcoin ensures that new coins will be minted at a fixed rate because the computational puzzles become more complex as the total computational resources devoted to coin generation increases.

Bitcoins can be divided and recombined to create essentially any denomination possible.

Bitcoin transactions quickly become irreversible, easing concerns which exist with credit card fraud and chargebacks.

"Bitcoin" refers to the network itself, while "bitcoin" refers to the currency.

bitcoin

The currency used and generated within the Bitcoin system. Abbreviated as "BTC" or "XBT". One bitcoin (BTC) is equal to 100,000,000 satoshis.

Bitcoin denominations

1 BTC = 1 Bitcoin = 100,000,000 satoshis

1 Centi-Bitcoin (cBTC or Bitcent) = 0.01 BTC

1 Milli-Bitcoin (mBit or millibit) = 0.001 BTC

1 Micro-Bitcoin (microbit or ubit) = 0.000.001 BTC

Bitcoin Investment Trust

A private, open-ended trust which invests exclusively in bitcoins and uses a state-of-the-art protocol to store the bitcoins on behalf of investors.

Provides a service where persons can invest in bitcoins without having to purchase and safely store the bitcoins themselves.

Bitcoin faucet

A website that gives away bitcoins to visitors for performing a simple task such as providing an email address, viewing a video, viewing a website, or playing a game.

Bitcoin Network

A network comprised of thousands of computers, all working to secure the network and confirm bitcoin transactions. Performing work on the Bitcoin Network by contributing hashing power is compensated with an award of bitcoins every 10 minutes and is awarded to only one party or mining pool at a time. The number of bitcoins awarded will decrease over time until all bitcoin have been created. At that time miners will be rewarded solely through transaction fees.

Bitcoin Protocol

The set of rules which govern miners. Establishes the increasing mining difficulty and award of bitcoins for performing hashing on the network.

Bitcoin wallet

The digital address where bitcoins are stored. Digital location where bitcoins are sent or received in a Bitcoin transaction.

Bitcoin 2.0

Bitcoin 2.0 takes Bitcoin's technologies and it to various other aspects of life such as smart contracts, asset transfers, corporations, web services, and government administration, for example.

Bitpay

A payment processor for bitcoins, which works with merchants, enabling them to accept bitcoins as payment.

BitShares

BitShares is a brand of **Distributed Autonomous Company**, (DAC). A DAC is a free market company whose shares can be transferred from person to person over the internet without any third party brokers. A DAC is not a legal entity or person like traditional companies, but exists entirely as a decentralized transaction ledger maintained by a network of individual computers owned by regular people all over the world.

Bitcoin is a single DAC which brands its shares as "coins" and markets them for use as a decentralized currency. The difference between BitShares and Bitcoin is that BitShares DACs are designed around profitable business models so their shares pay dividends, whereas, bitcoins are a currency which are continually debased to fund operations.

BitStamp

An exchange for bitcoins.

Block

This is the heart of the Bitcoin system.

Bitcoin is essentially an open ledger accounting system. Bitcoin transactions are broadcast to the network when they are made and then are recorded in a block by the miner who solved the most recent Bitcoin math problem. One block is like one page from that ledger, showing recent transactions that the network agrees are valid.

A block is a collection of transaction data, and one of the fundamental elements of cryptocurrency. A block is a data structure that consists of a **block header** and a **merkle tree** of transactions. Each block (except for the genesis block) references one previous block and thereby forms a tree called the **blockchain**. A block is therefore a group of transactions with a timestamp and a **proof-of-work** attached.

As transactions are made, the information is collected. When the gathered data reaches a predetermined size, it is bundled as a block. As soon as possible after a block is created, it is processed by investors for transaction verification in a process known as **mining**.

The point of bitcoin mining is to create blocks. The creator of a block is rewarded with bitcoins, the number of which decreases over time. The block creator is also awarded any transaction fees attached to the transactions included in the block. Eventually new blocks will stop creating bitcoins altogether and miners will be rewarded solely through transaction fees.

In order for a transaction to be confirmed its various components must be validated and checked against **double spending**. Once verified, transactions are incorporated in frequently issued official records called blocks. Anyone is allowed to create a block. In fact, two incentives are offered to attract verifiers to compete for block creation; the collection of fees and the minting of new coins.

Transactions become effective when they have been referenced in a block, which serves as the official record of executed transactions. Transactions can only be listed in a block if they satisfy such conditions as valid timestamping and absence of double spending.

A block consists of one "**coinbase**" minting transaction, zero or more regular spending transactions, a computational proof of work, and a reference to the chronologically prior block. Thus the blocks form a singly linked "blockchain" rooted in Nakamoto's genesis block whose hash is hardcoded in the software.

The regular creation of new blocks serves the dual purpose of ensuring the timely vetting of new transactions and the creation of new coins, all in a decentralized process driven by economic incentives (the minting of new coins and the collection of fees) balanced by computational costs. A feedback mechanism ensures an average block creation interval of ten minutes across the entire network.

Each block includes the difficult-to-produce verification hash of the previous block. This allows each subsequent block to be linked to all previous blocks.

Block Chain

The block chain is a public record of Bitcoin transactions in chronological order. The block chain is shared among all Bitcoin users. It is used to verify the permanence of Bitcoin transactions and to prevent double spending.

A block chain is the main chain, a single, most difficult chain of blocks. The block chain is updated by mining of new transactions. Unconfirmed transactions are not part of the block chain. If there is disagreement on which chain is main or which blocks are valid, a **fork** occurs.

Each block includes the difficult-to-produce verification hash of the previous block. This allows each subsequent block to be linked to all previous blocks, known as the block chain. As such, blocks of bitcoin transaction data does not stand alone. The data is created and processed and interlinked with other blocks to form the block chain.

On rare occasions errors in transaction data are not found immediately or in the block in which the information is embedded. However, as the processing, or mining, continues information in the block chain is reviewed repeatedly. As a result, the further down the chain a transaction is, the more secure and correct its details are.

If every block is a page of an accounting ledger, then the bottom of each page of the ledger would have a calculation based on the contents of that page that must be solved before the next page can be created. Because of the linking of the blocks together in this way, the validity of every page in the ledger can be confirmed since it links with the page before and behind it. Linking the blocks together makes it impossible to create deceptive blocks and allows the system to be trusted.

The block chain database is shared and available to all nodes participating in a cryptocurrency such as Bitcoin. With this information, one can determine how much value belonged to each address at any point in history.

Block Header

A data structure containing a previous block hash, a **hash** of a **merkle tree** of transactions, a **timestamp**, a **difficulty** and a **nonce**.

Block height

A sequence number of a block in a block chain. Height 0 refers to the genesis block. Several blocks may share the same height, (see **Orphan**), but only one of them belongs to the main chain.

Blockchain.info

A web service running a Bitcoin node and displaying statistics and raw data of all the transactions and blocks. The service also provides a web wallet functionality with lightweight clients for Android, iOS and OS X.

Block Reward

The reward given to a miner which has successfully hashed a transaction block. This can be a combination of coins and transaction fees, depending on the policy used by the cryptocurrency in question and whether all of the coins have been successfully mined. The block reward halves when a certain number of blocks have been mined. In Bitcoin's case the threshold is every 210,000 blocks, or approximately every four years. The block reward for Bitcoin was originally 50 bitcoins. Bitcoin currently awards 25 bitcoins for each block.

Bot Trading

The majority of investors in cryptocurrencies use manual methods when they want to buy, sell or trade. However, programs now exist for trading cryptocurrencies. Investors download these programs, which monitor cryptocurrency exchanges and markets. These "bots" execute transactions automatically according to the criterion the investor has set.

Brain Wallet

Refers to a concept of storing Bitcoins in one's own mind by memorizing a pass phrase. So long as the pass phrase is not recorded anywhere, the Bitcoins can be thought of as only existing in the mind of the holder.

The holder of the cryptocurrency stores a private keys as a memorable pharse without any digital or paper trace. Either a single key is used for a single address, or a deterministic wallet is derived from a single key.

A brain wallet greatly reduces the risk of theft. However it is prone to errors when the owner forgets the secret phrase, or the phrase is too simple and therefore prone to hacking. Additional risks result from required complex software.

Brainwallet.org

A web based utility to craft transactions by hand, convert private keys to addresses and work with a brain wallet.

Branching Point

The block at which the block chain diverges into multiple chain branches. The full list of blocks that have been mined since the start of the cryptocurrency. The block chain is designed so that each block contains a hash drawing on the blocks that came before it. This is designed to make the network more tamper proof.

BTC

The most popular currency code for 1 bitcoin.

Change

Informal name for a portion of a transaction output that is returned to the sender as a "change" after spending that output.

Since transaction outputs cannot be partially spent, one can spend 1 BTC out of 3 BTC output only by creating two new outputs: a "payment" output with one BTC sent to a payee address, and a "change" output with remaining 2 BTC (less transaction fees) sent to the payer's addresses.

BitcoinQT always uses new an address from a key pool for enhanced privacy. Blockchain.info sends to a default address in the wallet.

A common mistake when working with a paper wallet or a brain wallet is to make a change transaction to a different address and then accidentally delete it. For example, when importing a **private key** in a temporary BitcoinQT wallet, making a transaction and then deleting the temporary wallet which contains the change.

Checkpoint

Also known as "checkpoint lockin".

A very deep block (several days old) accepted by the overwhelming majority of users. Reorganization will not occur past that point.

Protects most of the history from a 51% attack. Since the checkpoints affect how the main chain is determined, they become part of the protocol and must be recognized by alternative nodes.

Cloud Mining

A relatively new mining process whereby hashing power is purchased on a mining rig that is housed and managed by others.

This allows investors to purchase hashing power at a competitive price without having the costs of hardware, maintenance, energy, upgrades, all of which are built into the contract price.

Cloud mining contracts are usually highly flexible, allowing the miner to choose the amount of hashing power and contract price that best suits them. The contracts typically carry the right to transfer to another miner.

Coinbase

A name for the transaction that produces new bitcoins. A block consists of one coinbase minting transaction, among other things. (See **Block**) Initially each new block awarded 50 bitcoins. The minting rate is programmed to decrease by half approximately every four years upon the verification of 210,000 blocks and at this writing sits at 25 bitcoins. The minting rate is programmed to reach zero when the total supply reaches 21 million bitcoins. The coinbase transaction also serves to claim all the fees in the transactions collected in the block. Both mining and fees motivate persons to create blocks and hence keep the system alive.

Also refers to the input script that generates new bitcoins. The input of such transactions contains some arbitrary data where the scriptSig would normally appear. This data is sometimes called the coinbase.

The Nakamoto genesis block transaction contains a reference to a *The Times* article from January 3, 2009 to prove that more blocks were not created before that date. Some mining pools put their names in the coinbase as a means to estimate how much hash rate each pool produces.

Coinbase is also used to vote on a protocol change. (An example is Pay-to Script Hash.) Miners vote by putting some agreed upon marker in the coinbase. If a majority of miners support it and expect non-mining users to accept it, then they simply start enforcing the new rule. The minority must then choose to continue with a forked block chain, thus producing a new altcoin, or accept the new rule.

Coinbase.com

United States based bitcoin/USD exchange and web wallet service.

Coin Age

The length of time since a coin has last been spent.

Noting how long since a number of coins have been transacted is one indication of the velocity of bitcoins in the Bitcoin economy.

Colored Coin

A concept of adding a special meaning to certain Bitcoin transaction outputs. This could be used to create a tradeable commodity on top of Bitcoin protocol.

This is a project of BitcoinX to allow for the "marking" of some bitcoins so that they can be used for specific purposes like stocks, contracts, and even physical property. The project is under development and is one of many attempts to build more practical applications on top of the Bitcoin protocol and to further increase its utility beyond currency or a store of value.

A salient and very innovative feature of Bitcoin is allowing users (payers and payees) to embed scripts in their Bitcoin transactions. In theory one can realize rich transactional semantics and contracts through scripts, such as deposits, escrow and dispute mediation, insurance contracts, including the use of external states, and so on. It is conceivable that in the future, richer forms of financial contracts and mechanisms are going to be built around Bitcoin using this feature.

For example, a company may create 1 million shares and declare a single transaction output containing 10 bitcoins as a source of these shares. Then, some or all of these bitcoins can be moved to other addresses, sold or exchanged. While voting or distributing dividends, share owners could then prove ownership by signing a specific message by the **private key** associated with the addresses holding bitcoins derived from the initial source.

Cold Storage

A collective term for various security measures to reduce the risk of remote or unauthorized access to private keys. It could be a personal computer disconnected from the internet, a dedicated hardware wallet, a USB stick with a wallet file, or a paper wallet.

Compact Size

Original name of a variable-length integer format used in transaction and block serialization. Also known as "Satoshi's encoding".

This format uses 1, 3, 5 or 9 bytes to represent a 64-bit insigned integer. Values lower than 253 are represented with 1 byte. Bytes 253, 254 and 255 indicate a 16-, 32- or 64-bit integer follows.

Confirmation / Confirmed Transaction

Refers to an event whereby a transaction has been processed by the network and is highly unlikely to be reversed.

When a transaction is successfully entered into a block, it is said to be "confirmed". This means that more than 51% of the Bitcoin nodes recognize that the transaction is valid and that there has been no attempt to **double spend** those bitcoins.

Transactions receive a confirmation when they are included in a block. Although a single confirmation can be considered secure for low value transactions, it is advisable to wait for **6 confirmations** or more. Each confirmation exponentially decreases the risk of a reversed transaction. 6 confirmations are generally enough to make the validy of a transaction beyond question.

To protect against double spending, a transaction should not be considered as "confirmed" until a certain number of blocks in the block chain verify the transaction. The classic Bitcoin client will show a transaction as "n/unconfirmed" until 6 blocks verify the transaction.

Confirmation Number

A measure of probability that a transaction could be rejected from the main chain.

"**Zero confirmations**" means that transaction is unconfirmed (not yet in a block). "One confirmation" means that the transaction is included in the latest block in the main chain. "Two confirmations" means that the transaction is included in the block right before the latest one; and so on. The probability of a transaction being reversed is diminished exponentially as more blocks are added "on top" of it.

CPU

Acronym for "central processing unit". This is the brains of any computer and handles most calculations on a day-to-day basis for basis computer functions.

In the early days of bitcoin mining, miners utilized the computational power of their CPUs to mine bitcoins. This was soon surpassed by GPU mining technology as mining difficulty increased to a point where CPU mining was no longer profitable.

Cryptocurrency

"Crypto" derives from Greek for "hidden" or "to hide".

A form of currency solely based on mathematics. Unlike fiat currency, which is printed, cryptocurrency is produced by solving mathematical problems based on cryptography.

As a digital currency, cryptocurrency relies on an open source cryptography protocol to manage its distribution and transactions, rather than a centralized authority such as a government or a central bank. A cryptocurrency is therefore not subject to inflation, regulation or fees and other charges that affect typical traditional currencies.

Cryptocurrencies are relatively new. The first to be publicly introduced was Bitcoin in 2009.

The security of these networks is ensured by the strength of the cryptography used.

Cryptography

The process of coding written messages with the use of mathematics to create codes and ciphers that can conceal information. Used to create mathematical proofs that provide high levels of security. The basis for the mathematical problems used to verify and secure Bitcoin transactions. Online commerce and banking also use cryptography.

In the case of Bitcoin, cryptography is used, for example, to make it impossible for someone to spend funds in another's wallet or to corrupt the block chain. It is also used to encrypt a wallet so that it cannot be breached without a password.

Deflation

The reduction of prices in an economy over time. Occurs when the supply of goods and services increases faster than the supply of money, or when the supply of money is finite and spending decreases. This leads to more goods or services per unit of currency, requiring less currency to purchase them.

Deflation, according to some, is undesirable. When people expect prices to fall, they stop spending and hoard money in the hope that their money will go further in the near future. This phenomena can depress an economy.

On the other hand, a deflationary currency will reward saving, allow salaries to naturally increase in value, and make financial planning more certain. A deflationary currency favors those furthest from the money supply, which may explain why politicians, economists and bankers tend to oppose the idea.

Most currencies in circulation today are inflationary. Governments produce more money to pay their debts. The increased money supply drives prices up. When the supply of a currency is finite, (such as bitcoins), its value will adjust to demand, and in most cases the costs of goods and services will tend to go down.

Denial of Service (DoS)

A form of attack on the network. Bitcoin nodes punish certain behavior of other nodes by banning their IP addresses for 24 hours to avoid DoS. Also, some theoretical attacks, like 51% attack, may be used for network-wide DoS.

Depth

Refers to a place in the **blockchain**. A transaction with **6 confirmations** can also be referred to as "6 blocks deep".

Deterministic Wallet

A collective term for different ways to generate a sequence of private keys and/or public keys. A deterministic wallet does not need a Key Pool.

The simplest form of a deterministic wallet is based on hashing a secret string linked together with a key number. For each number the resulting hash is used as a private key (the public key is derived from it). More complex schemes use elliptic curve arithmetic to derive sequences of public and private keys separately which allows generating new addresses for every payment request without storing private keys on a web server.

Difficulty

This is a measure of how difficult it is to find a new block compared to the easiest it can ever be. By definition it is the maximum target divided by the current target.

This number determines how difficult it is to hash a new block. It is related to the maximum allowed number in a given numerical portion of a transaction block's hash. The lower the number, the more difficult it is to produce a hash value that fits it.

Difficulty varies based on the amount of computing power used by miners on the Bitcoin network. If large numbers of miners leave the network, the difficulty would decrease. Thus far, however, Bitcoin's growing popularity has attracted more computing power to the network, meaning the difficulty has increased.

Difficulty is used in two Bitcoin rules: 1) every block must meet a difficulty target to ensure a ten minute interval between blocks and 2) transactions are considered confirmed only when belonging to a main chain which is the one with the biggest cumulative difficulty of all blocks. As of September 5, 2013 the difficulty was 86 933 018 and grows by 20-30% every two weeks.

On average, a block is produced every ten minutes. However, the number of miners and the amount of computing power does not remain constant. As Bitcoin becomes more popular, greater computing power means a reduction in the amount of time it takes to produce a block. Therefore, at regular periods, the difficulty of the problems miners must solve to produce a block is recalculated to keep the rate of block production at about ten minutes.

Every 2016 blocks, Bitcoin adjusts the difficulty of verifying blocks based on the time it took to verify the previous 2016 blocks. The difficulty is adjusted so that given the average estimated computing power of the entire Bitcoin network, only one block will be verified on average every ten minutes for the next 2016 blocks.

The difficulty is usually expressed as a number, optionally accurate to many decimal places. (For example, in block 100,000 the difficulty was expressed as 14,484.162361.) The difficulty is inversely proportional to the hash target, which is expressed as a hex number with approximately 50 digits, and is the number under which a block's generated hash must be to qualify as an officially verified block. The hash target is equal to $((65535 << 208 / difficulty)$.

Mining consists of attempting to find a hash of: the previous block, the current set of un-blocked transactions, a transaction indicating where the block reward plus fees should be paid, and a **nonce** (number once used).

Since any change to the **nonce** will randomly change the resulting hash, mining involves trying trillions of different nonce values in order to find a hash that is numerically below the current difficulty number, thereby solving the block. In theory the first hash tried could solve the current block. But that is unlikely in practice.

Every hash has an equal chance of solving a block. So, while there is an average time to solve a block, theoretically there is no limit to the length of time it might take to solve a block.

Difficulty is also often called block difficulty, hash difficulty, verification difficulty, or the difficulty of generating bitcoins.

Digital Signatures

A **hash** of a document encrypted with a **private key**.

When the digital signature is attached to the document, then anyone with the **public key** can create their own hash of that document, decrypt the original hash using the public key, and compare. If the hashes match, then it can be concluded that the document sender is confirmed and the document has not been altered. Otherwise the decrypted hash would not match the generated hash.

Distributed Autonomous Company

A software entity that, like a traditional company, earns money for its shareholders. Unlike a traditional company, it operates autonomously on a blockchain. It requires no board of directors or CEO to accomplish its goals.

A DAC requires no trust in people as its rules are written into software.

Double spending

An attempt to spend the same transaction output twice.

There are two major ways to perform a double spend: (1) reverting an unconfirmed transaction by making another one which has a higher chance of being included in a block. This only works with merchants accepting zero-confirmation transactions, or (2) by mining a parallel block chain with a second transaction to overtake the chain where the first transaction was included.

The Bitcoin **proof-of-work** scheme, virtually guarantees the prevention of double spend transactions recorded in the blockchain. The deeper the transaction is recorded in the **blockchain**, the more expensive it is to "reverse" it.

If someone tries to spend the same bitcoins at two different places at the same time, one transaction would be recorded in a block and confirmed and the other would be considered non-valid and thereby deprive the intended recipient the bitcoins.

As the transaction gains in confirmations, the risk of a double spend decreases.

Although possible, double spends would not be worth the effort in small transactions and those conducting large transactions would certainly be willing to wait for 1-6 confirmations.

Double spending is not easy to do, but it is nevertheless a risk run by those choosing to accept **zero-confirmation** transactions. Bitcoin mining and the block chain are there to create a consensus on the network about which of the two transactions will confirm and be considered valid.

See also **51% attack**.

Dust

A transaction output that is smaller than a typical fee required to spend it. This is not a strict part of the protocol, as any amount more than zero is valid.

A bitcoin can be divided into one-hundred million pieces, known as **satoshis**. Very small denominations of bitcoins are known as dust as they have no practical value. Some websites, such as **faucets**, may attempt to make many dust transactions, which clutter up the block chain. Small transaction fees and limits on how many satoshis can be sent have been imposed to limit dust transactions. Refusal to mine or relay dust transactions has been imposed to avoid unnecessarily increasing the size of **unspent transaction outputs (UXTO)** index.

See **UXTO**.

ECDSA

The **Elliptic Curve Digital Signature Algorithm** is a lightweight cryptographic algorithm used to sign transactions in the Bitcoin protocol. It is used to verify transaction ownership when making a transfer of bitcoins.

See Signature

Elliptic Curve Arithmetic

A set of mathematical operations defined on a group of points on a 2D elliptical curve. Bitcoin protocol uses a predefined curve secp256k1.

Escrow

Escrow is the act of letting a third party hold the money during a transaction until both parties agree that all transaction terms have been successfully completed. With Bitcoin, transactions are irreversible and so requests that funds be held in escrow should be expected.

It has been suggested that escrows could become automated with apps built on top of the Bitcoin protocol. Funds would be sent to a particular address and would not be released until certain conditions that could be automatically checked are met.

Ethereum

A next-generation cryptocurrency and decentralized application platform.

A so-called "Bitcoin 2.0" protocol inspired by Bitcoin which intend to make the underlying technology usable for far more than just currency.

Exchange

An Exchange is a business where one currency is converted into another. Cryptocurrency Exchanges may swap between different cryptocurrencies and fiat currencies.

Bitcoin Exchanges have had a number of difficulties gaining financial and legal footing, making the exchange of fiat and bitcoin tricky.

Extra Nonce

A number placed in coinbase script and incremented by a miner each time the nonce 32-bit integer overflows.

This is not the required way to continue mining when **nonce** overflows. One can also change the **merkle tree** of transactions or change a **public key** used for collecting a block reward.

See **Nonce**.

Faucet

A technique used when first launching an **altcoin**. A set number of coins are pre-mined and given away for free to encourage people to take interest in the coin and begin mining it themselves.

Though the amounts given away are small, faucets teach people about Bitcoin and other altcoins and help them become comfortable using wallets without having to risk their own money

Fiat currency

Money conjured out of thin air by government decree. It has value because the government says it does by legal decree by requiring it be accepted. Its primary utility is in dealing with the government. Usually inflationary and subject to broad manipulation by the issuing authority.

Governments prefer fiat money to manage its debt. By issuing more fiat the government causes inflation which drives down the relative value of its debt. This benefits the government and the banks at the expense of everyone else.

Constantly under close scrutiny by government regulators due to its known application in money laundering and terrorist activities. Not to be confused with bitcoin.

FPGA

Acronym for "field-programmable gate array".

This is a computer chip which is intended to be customized by the end user; miners in the case of Bitcoin. A FPGA can be configured with custom functions after it has been fabricated. Think of it as a blank silicon slate on which instructions can be written.

This was the next evolution in Bitcoin mining hardware after GPU miners. FPGA offers far greater hashing power and efficiency than GPUs. Because FPGAs can be mass produced and configured after fabrication, manufacturers benefit from economies of scale, making them cheaper than ASIC chips. However, they are usually far slower. FPGA technology is being superseded by ASIC mining rigs.

FinCEN

The Financial Crimes Enforcement Network, an agency within the United States Treasury Department. FinCEN has thus far been the main organization to impose regulations on exchanges trading in bitcoin.

Fork

A fork occurs when two blocks dealing with the same transaction are produced. In such a case, one set of miners will be working off one block, while another set of miners work off the other block.

Can refer to a fork in the source code to create a new **altcoin** or, more often, to a split of the **blockchain** when two different parts of the network see different main chains.

A fork occurs every time two blocks of the same height are created at the same time. Both blocks always have different hashes, and therefore different difficulty, so that when a node recognizes both of them, it will always choose the most difficult one. However, before both blocks arrive to a majority of nodes, two parts of the network will see different blocks as tips of the main chain.

Forks occur in the case of 51% attacks, because of bugs in the protocol or because core developers wish to introduce a new feature into the protocol.

There have been several successful forks due to developers

introducing features and one as a result of a bug. In the case of the bug, the bug was quickly recognized and the mining community rallied to accept the correct fork with a fix to the bug.

Full Node

A node which implements all of Bitcoin protocol and does not require trusting any external service to validate transactions. It is able to download and validate the entire **blockchain**.

All full nodes implement the same peer-to-peer messaging protocol to exchange transactions and blocks, but that is not a requirement.

A full node may receive and validate data using any protocol and from any source. However, the highest security is achieved by being able to communicate as fast as possible with as many nodes as possible.

Genesis Block

The very first block in the block chain mined by **Satoshi Nakamoto** that began it all with hard-coded contents and an all-zero reference to a previous block.

Genesis block was released on January 3, 2009 with a newspaper quote in its **coinbase**: "The Times 03/Jan/2009 Chancellor on brink of second bailout for banks" as proof that there was no secretly pre-minted blocks to overtake the block chain in the future. The message ironically refers to a reason for Bitcoin existence: a constant inflation of money supply by government and central banks.

Generate bitcoins

When a bitcoin miner finds a block, it receives newly minted bitcoins and the transaction fees which may or may not be included in the block. The amount of bitcoins awarded for verifying a block is 50 BTC for the first 210,000 blocks and half the previous amount of bitcoins for each subsequent 210,000 blocks.

On the average, 210,000 blocks take about 4 years to verify. The total amount of bitcoins that will ever be mined in 21,000,000 BTC.

Gigahashes/sec

The number of hashing attempts possible in a given second, measured in billions of hashes (thousands of Megahashes).

GPU

Acronym for "graphical processing unit".

This is an early generation technology used for bitcoin mining. Miners found that GPUs could hash algorithms on the Bitcoin network far faster than CPUs leading to the first major shift of bitcoin mining hardware.

In the formative days of bitcoin mining, bitcoins were mined with regular computers. Soon after, it was discovered that the GPUs used for gaming were more efficient. Most miners switched to GPUs before transitioning to ASICs.

Halving

Refers to reducing the mining reward every 210,000 blocks (approximately every 4 years).

From the genesis block to block 209999 in December 2012, the reward was 50 BTC. From then until 2016 the reward will be 25 BTC, and so on until 1 satoshi will be rewarded in the year 2140. After that point no more bitcoins will ever be created.

Due to reward halving, the total supply of bitcoins is finite; only about 2100 trillion satoshis will ever be created.

Hard Fork

A term used to stress that changing Bitcoin protocol requires overwhelming majority to agree with the change.

Hash

1. A mathematical process which turns a large amount of data into a

short, fixed-length output.

2. A checksum value unique to the underlying data. This sum is being searched by all the miners attempting to process a cryptographic block to be returned to the cryptographic network as a "proof of work". The first miner to submit the correct proof of work is what initiates the creation and awarding on new coins to the successful miner.

This is the random and complex mathematical formula used in the verification of blocks of transaction data in the process known as mining.

Once the miner calculates the proper hash in a block, it is rewarded with coins and a percentage of the transaction fees embedded in that block.

Achieving the right hash in a given block can take several tries and calculation adjustments. Some blocks, even though properly processed, may not "pay out".

The difficulty of calculating the hash in a block is set fairly high so that the rewards are not distributed to quickly. Mining helps create new coins and the mathematics is set so that the creation of new coins does not happen too quickly so as to destabilize the currency.

Hashes are useful to Bitcoin because it is mathematically difficult to work out what the original input was by looking at the output. Furthermore, changing even the tiniest part of the input will produce an entirely different output.

Hashing

The computational activity a miner carries out on a cryptographic network such as Bitcoin.

Hash function

A computer algorithm designed to take any arbitrary input of any length and produce a numeric derivative of that input, known as the data's "hash". These can be used to easily verify that the data has not been altered. If a single bit of the original data is changed and the hash algorithm is run, the hash will completely change.

Because the hash is seemingly random, it is prohibitively difficult to try to produce a specific hash by changing the data which is being hashed.

Bitcoin uses two cryptographic hash functions; **SHA-256**, which produces a 256bit hash, and RIPEMD-160. SHA-256 is used almost exclusively in two round hashing (Hash256). RIPEMD-160 is only used in computing an address (see also **Hash160**). Scripts may use not only Hash 256 and Hash160, but also SHA-1, SHA-256 and RIPEMD-160.

Hash160

SHA-256 hashed with RIPEMD-160. It is used to produce an address because it makes a smaller hash (20 bytes vs 32 bytes) than SHA-256, but still uses SHA-256 for internally for security.

It is known as BTCHash160() in CoreBitcoin, Hash160() in BitcoinQT. It is also available in scriptsas OP_HASH160.

Hash256

When not speaking of arbitrary hash functions, Hash refers to two rounds of **SHA-256**. That is, compute a SHA-256 hash of the data followed by another SHA-256 of that hash.

This process is used in block header hashing, transaction hashing, creating a **merkle tree** of transactions, or computing a checksum of an **address**.

It is known as BTCHash256() in CoreBitcoin, Hash() in BitcoinQT. It is also available is scripts as OP_HASH256.

(To) Hash

The act of computing a hash function of some data.

Hash rate

The number of hashes that can be performed by a bitcoin miner in a given period of time, (usually one second).

A measure of mining hardware performance expressed in hashes per second. It is the measuring unit of the processing power of the Bitcoin network. The Bitcoin network must make intensive mathematical operations for security purposes. When the network reached a hash rate of 10 Th/s, the network could perform 10 trillion calculations per second.

The hash rate necessary to successfully mine a block has been rising exponentially.

Presently, the hash rate of all bitcoin mining nodes combined is approximately 647,000 gigahashes per second (Gh/s). For comaprison, AMD Radeon graphics cards produce from 200 to 800 megahashes per second (Mh/s) depending on the model.

Hash Type (hashtype)

A single byte appended to a transaction signature in the transaction inout which describes how the transaction should be hashed in order to verify that signature.

Three types affecting outputs exist: ALL (default), SINGLE, NONE and one optional modifier ANYONECANPAY affecting the inputs and can be combined with either of the first three.

ALL requires all outputs to be hashed. Thus, all outputs are signed.

SINGLE clears all output scripts but the one with the same index as the input in question.

NONE clears all outputs, thus allowing changes at will.

ANYONECANPAY removes all inputs except the current which allows anyone to contribute independently.

The actual behavior is more subtle than this overview, so one should check the actual source code for more comments.

Hybrid wallet

A cryptocurrency storage and maintenance system that is a

combination of a software wallet (stored on a private computer) and a web wallet (stored on a third-party server).

The bulk of the digital currency account information is stored on the wallet host's server – except for one important detail. The private key (the code that uniquely identifies the owner) is stored only on the private device. During a transaction, the private key is encrypted on the way to the exchange's server, so the private key is never revealed.

Access to the **private key** also includes a password that only the owner knows.

Inflation

A decrease in the value of money over time, resulting in a rise in the prices of goods and services. The result is a drop in the purchasing power of money. The effects are less incentive to save money and more motivation to spend it quickly before prices increase.

Results from the loss of confidence in a currency or currency manipulation.

Input

Denotes where a Bitcoin payment has originated. Typically this will be a Bitcoin address, unless the transaction is a generation transaction, meaning that the bitcoin has been freshly minted.

Invalid block

A **block** is "valid" if it obeys all of the Protocol rules; otherwise it is "invalid". Clients will ignore invalid blocks when determining which chain is difficulty-wise-longest. Mining clients will not build on top of invalid blocks.

The **block chain** that represents the entire history of all transactions in the Bitcoin network is linear; there can be no [permanent] branches. If two miners solve a block at about the same time, a branch occurs, and miners may begin building on either of the two. The block chain which grows faster becomes the "valid" block chain for the network and the blocks in the losing chain become invalid. Thus there is a 100-block maturation time before block rewards and transaction fees may be spent. It acts as insurance against those BTC becoming invalid in the meantime.

Key

May refer to an ECDSA public or private key, or AES symmetric encryption key.

AES is not used in the Bitcoin protocol itself, but is used only to encrypt the ECDSA keys and other sensitive data, so "key" usually refers to an ECDSA key.

Usually refers to a private key as a public key can always be derived from a private key.

Key pool

Some wallet applications that create new private keys randomly keep a pool of unused pre-generated keys. (Bitcoin QT keeps 100 keys by default.)

When a new key is required for a change of address or new payment request, the application provides the oldest key from pool and replaces it with a fresh new one.

The purpose of the pool is to ensure that recently used keys are always backed up on external storage. A key pool guarantees that a key was backed up several days before being assigned.

Kilohash

1000 hashes

KYC

"Know Your Client" rules force financial institutions to vet their customers to ensure no money laundering is taking place.

Lightweight client

Unlike a full node, a lightweight node does not store the entire block chain and therefore cannot fully verify any transaction.

Two types of lightweight nodes exist: those fully trusting an external service to determine wallet balance and validity of transactions (eg block chain information) and the apps implementing **Simplified Payment Verification (SPV).**

SPV clients do not need to trust any particular service, but are more vulnerable to a 51% attack than full nodes.

Legal tender

Currency issued by authority of a government that may be lawfully tendered in payment of a debt. Includes paper money, Federal Reserve notes, or coins. Must be accepted by a creditor if offered in payment of a debt.

The pertinent portion of U.S. Law is the Coinage Act of 1965, specifically Section 31 U.S.C. 5103, entitled "Legal tender", which states: "United States coins and currency (including Federal Reserve notes and circulating notes of Federal Reserve banks and national banks) are legal tender for all debts, public charges, taxes and dues."

Therefore, all United States currency identified in the statute are a valid and legal offer payment for debts when tendered to a creditor. There is not, however, a Federal statute mandating that a private business, a person or an organization must accept currency or coins for payment of goods and services.

Private businesses are free to develop their own policies on whether or not to accept legal tender unless there is a State law which states otherwise. For example, a bus line may prohibit payment of fares in pennies or dollar bills. In addition, movie theaters, convenience stores and gas stations may refuse to accept large denomination currency as a matter of policy.

Litecoin

An **altcoin** based on the **Scrypt** mining algorithm and is mined by the **proof-of-work** method.

Introduced to the public in October 2011. Was the first major cryptocurrency produced since the introduction of bitcoin in 2009.

Despite the introduction of many new cryptocurrencies since that time, Litecoin holds the number two spot in in popularity behind bitcoin.

Lock Time (locktime)

A 32-bit field in a transaction that means either a block height at which the transaction becomes valid, or a UNIX timestamp. "Zero" means the transaction is valid in any block. A number less than 500000000 is intrepreted as a block number (the limit will be hit after year 11000), otherwise a timestamp.

mBTC

A millibitcoin, or one thousandth of a bitcoin (0.001BTC). Often referred to as a "milli".

Mhash/J

Millions of hashes per joule. Measures energy efficiency.

Mhash/s

Millions of hashes per second. Measures raw speed performance.

Mainnet

Main Bitcoin network and its block chain. The term is used most often in comparison to **testnet**.

Main Chain

A portion of the **block chain** which a **node** considers the most difficult. All nodes store all valid blocks, including orphans, and re-compute the total difficulty when receiving another block. If the newly arrived block or blocks do not extend the existing main chain but create another one from some previous block, it is called a reorganization.

Memory Pool

Generators store transaction waiting to get into a block in their memory pool after receiving them. Received transactions are stored even if they are invalid to prevent nodes from constantly requesting transactions that they have already seen. The memory pool is cleared when Bitcoin is shut down, causing the network to gradually forget about transactions that haven't been included in a block.

Mempool

See **Memory Pool**. A technical term for a collection of unconfirmed transactions stored by a **node** until they either expire or are included in the main chain.

When reorganization occurs, transactions from orphaned blocks either become invalid (if already included in the main chain) or moved to a pool of unconfirmed transactions. By default, bitcoin nodes dispose of unconfirmed transactions after 24 hours.

Merkle root

Every transaction has a **hash** associated with it. In a block, all of the transaction hashes in the block are themselves hashed (sometimes several times – the exact process is complex), and the result is the Merkle root.

In other words, the Merkle root is the **hash** of all the hashes of all the transactions in the **block**.

The Merkle root is included in the **block header**. It is therefore possible to securely verify that a transaction has been accepted by the network (and get the number of confirmations) by downloading just the tiny **block headers** and **Merkle tree** – downloading the entire block chain is unnecessary. This feature is currently not used in Bitcoin, but it may in the future.

Merkle tree

An abstract data structure that organizes a list of data items in a tree of their hashes (such as Git, Mercurial or ZFS). In Bitcoin, the merkle tree is used only to organize transactions within a block (the block header contains only one hash of a tree) so that full nodes may prune fully spent transactions to save disk space. **SPV** clients store only block headers and validate transactions if they are provided with a list of all intermediate hashes.

Microtransaction

Paying a tiny amount for an asset or service, primarily online. In sales or exchanges on the internet, microtransactions are nearly impossible under conventional payment systems because of heavy commissions and fees. It is difficult to pay two cents to read an online article using a credit card, for example.

Miner

Computer software which is designed to repeatedly calculate hashes with the intention to create a successful block and earn coins from transaction fees and new coins created with the block itself.

The term references an analogy of gold miners who dig gold out of the ground and thus "discover new gold" that can be used to create new coins. A similar "discovery" occurs with a successful hash to create new bitcoins.

Those who attempt to earn bitcoins by performing useful work for the Bitcoin network.

Miners are rewarded for their efforts with blocks of bitcoins if they successfully perform calculations faster than their competitors.

Solo mining has become very challenging. Most miners choose to add their resources to a **Mining Pool** to greatly enhance the chances of finding and solving a valid block to mine bitcoins.

Mining

The act of generating new bitcoins by solving cryptographic problems using computing hardware.

Transaction record, also known as mining, is the process of adding transaction records to Bitcoin's journal of past transactions, also know as the **block chain**. The block chain serves to confirm its transactions to the rest of the network. Through this public journal, Bitcoin nodes can distinguish legitimate bitcoin transactions from attempts to re-spend coins that have already been spent elsewhere.

Cryptocurrency transactions are bundled together in packets of data called "blocks". The timely processing of these blocks is essential to the health of cryptocurrency. There is no central entity that can carry out the necessary processing, so the processing is delegated to the currency's investors. This is called "mining". The miners are offered incentives to take on the mining task.

Computer hardware performs mathematical calculations for the Bitcoin network to confirm transactions and increase security.

When a block of data is properly mined and specific predetermined algorithmic and mathematical criteria (collectively known as "**hash**") have been met, the miner collects a reward of coins and transaction fees from the block the miner has processed.

It is not required that one mine a cryptocurrency to invest in it.

Mining serves a dual purpose. Mining validates transactions which results in the generation of new currency.

Mining caps in Bitcoin means that the mining reward of coins will be phased out. When the cap is reached it is projected that transaction volume will be high enough to provide adequate incentive for miners to continue to take part in the process solely for a portion of the transaction fees.

Mining is a process of finding valid hashes of a block header by iterating millions of variants of block headers (using **nonce** and **extra nonce**) in order to find a hash lower than the target. The process is required to determine a single global history of all transactions grouped in blocks.

Mining consumes time and electricity. At the present time, the difficulty of mining is so great that energy-wise it is not profitable to mine using video graphic cards.

Mining is compensated with the award of transaction fees and block rewards of newly generated coins.

For the Bitcoin Network, the term "mining" was coined because of the similarity bitcoin production has to gold mining. This nomenclature is inaccurate in that winning one block is not like striking a vein of gold. Rather, in this respect, bitcoin mining is similar to a lottery wherein each hash is a ticket to win. Increasing hash power does not increase the supply of bitcoins, but merely increases the chance that the miner will win the next block.

Mining is a specialized and competitive market where the rewards are divided according to how much calculation is done. Mining is a very difficult process. Not all bitcoin users or investors mine coins.

Mining Difficulty

This refers to the probability that any particular calculation will find and solve a valid cryptographic block that generates bitcoins.

The Bitcoin network is designed to generate one of these blocks approximately every 10 minutes. As more miners and computing resources are applied to the network, the difficulty in finding a valuable block is automatically increased. This prevents the increased resources from finding a block in less than the desired 10 minute period to maintain the steady drip of bitcoins entering circulation.

Mining Pool

A group of miners who have chosen to join their computing resources to increase their collective hashing power and probability of finding and successfully processing a valid cryptographic block that will reward the miner with bitcoins and transaction fees.

The process of mining can require major resources of time, electricity and computer resources. Miners who desire efficiency will join together to apportion the processing burden.

Since the probability of finding a valid block hash is proportional to the miner's hashrate, small miners may have to work for a very long time before finding a block reward.

When more than one miner is involved in the processing of data blocks, this is called a mining pool. Once the mining is completed and verified, the pool's members divide the coin and transaction fee rewards proportionately. A miner's "share" are hashes that are numerically below a much lesser difficulty level than the block difficulty and would otherwise be useless but for the support of the pool. The pool can easily verify a miner's share hash is valid for a block which in turn proves the miner's work on the pool's block and through share quantity gives a reasonably accurate depiction of how much work the miner contributed to the pool's results.

Mining pools allow for a steady stream of income for miners which is distributed to the pool members.

Mining Rig

The computer system used to carry out the computational work of Bitcoin, Because of the increaasing computational difficulty inherent in Bitcoin, these machines have evolved and are custom built to perform this specialized computing in order to maximize efficiency and the probability of a mining operation.

Mixing, Mixing Service

Despite broad claims to the contrary, Bitcoin is not fully anonymous. All Bitcoin transactions are public and viewable on the **block chain**. It is therefore possible to trace bitcoins and transaction histories.

Mixing services are sites that pools a great many bitcoins together and then issue back bitcoins of an equal value. The mixing service mixes one's bitcoins with someone else's and returns bitcoins with different inputs and outputs. From the one's sent in. This randomizes the bitcoin histories and makes it much more difficult to track them. The process of exchanging coins among other persons increases the privacy of one's transaction history.

A mixing service (also known as a "tumbler") preserves one's privacy because it prevents others from tracing a particular bitcoin to an individual owner.

In traditional banking, a bank protects a customer's privacy by hiding transactions from all third parties. With Bitcoin any merchant could do a statistical analysis of a customer's entire payment history and determine, for instance, how many bitcoins the customer owns. While it is still possible to implement Know Your Customer (KYC) rules on a level of every merchant, mixing allows one to separate information about one's history between merchants.

Mintage Cap

As cryptocurrency miners process blocks of transaction data, new coins are generated. Cryptocurrencies are a new industry. Issuers want enough coins mined to satisfy new investors. New coins are mathematically designed to be turned out at a stable rate so that the value of the currency will remain relatively stable.

Over time the mathematics of coin creation is programmed to end. The intent is to avoid over saturation of the market and prevent currency devaluation. Production of most cryptocurrencies will cease when are predetermined number, known as the mintage cap is reached. When the last coin is mined, there will be no more new coins.

M-of-N Multi-signature Transaction

A transaction that can be spent using M signatures when N public keys are required (M is less than or equal to N). Multi-signature transactions that only contain one OP_CHECKMULTISIG opcode and N is 3, 2 or 1 are considered standard.

Node

A computer connected to the Bitcoin network using a client that relays transactions to others. Each Bitcoin client currently running within the network is referred to as a "node" of the system. These computers transmit transactions throughout the network.

Also referred to as a "client" of the system.

There are "full nodes" which are capable of validating the entire block chain and "lightweight nodes", with reduced functionality. Wallet applications which speak to a server are not considered nodes.

Nonce

Stands for "number used once". A 32-bit number in a block header which is iterated during a search for proof-of-work. It is an otherwise meaningless number which is used to alter the outcome of a hash.

A nonce is used to try and produce a digest that fits the numerical parameters set by the Bitcoin difficulty. A different nonce will be used with each hashing attempt, meaning that billions of nonces are generated when attempting to hash each transaction block.

Each time Bitcoin hashes a block, it increments a nonce within the block it is trying to verify. If the numeric value of the effectively random hash is below a certain amount determined by the block generation difficulty, then the block is accepted by other clients and is added to the chain.

Using a nonce ensures that the hash calculation is cryptographically secure (cannot be hacked) since it cannot be repeated without that random number.

Each time the nonce is changed, the hash of the block header is recalculated. If nonce overflows before valid **proof-of-work** is found, an extra nonce is incremented and placed in the **coinbase** script. Alternatively, one may change a **merkle tree** of transactions or a **timestamp**.

Orphan, Orphaned, Block

A valid block that is no longer part of a main chain. This usually happens when two or more blocks of the same height are produced at the same time. When one of them becomes a part of the main chain, others are considered "orphaned".

Orphans may also occur when the blockchain is forked due to an attack (see **51% attack**) or a bug. Then a chain of several blocks may become abandoned.

In the event that the **blockchain** is forked, an orphan block is on the chain that is abandoned for the main chain.

Offline Storage

This concept relates to how one's cryptocurrency is stored.

If the currency is online, on an active drive that is turned on, or accessible through cloud computing, it is also accessible to other computer users. That access can take place without the knowledge of the holder of the cryptocurrency. This can lead to hacking and theft since cryptocurrency by design is not connected directly to any one person.

As such it is important to maintain unique currency information offline as often as possible and to do so always except when the currency is directly in use for a transaction.

Two of the best ways to keep currency information offline is to store it in an external drive that is disconnected from any computer when it is not needed or to print it out or store it in a paper wallet.

If using a wallet service of a cryptocurrency exchange, it is advisable to determine whether the information is stored offline.

Digital currency theft is usually untraceable and irreversible.

Output

The destination address or addresses for a Bitcoin transaction.

Contains an amount to be sent and a script that allows further spending. The script usually contains a **public key** and a signature verification opcode. Only an owner of a corresponding **private key** is able to create another transaction that sends that amount further to someone else.

In every transaction, the sum of output amounts must be equal or less than the sum of all input amounts.

Paper Wallet

A form of **cold storage** where a **private key** for Bitcoin address is printed on a piece of paper (with or without encryption). As such, all traces of the key are removed from the computer where it was generated.

Bitcoin wallets need two strings of code; a **public key** identifying where the bitcoins will be stored and a **private key** which allows the owner to send those coins to a different address. A paper wallet is a printout of both these numbers either as strings of digits and letters or as **QR codes**.

To redeem bitcoins, a key must be imported in the wallet application so it can sign a transaction.

If created properly, paper wallets are considered one of the most secure ways to store cryptocurrencies.

Pay-to-Script Hash, P2SH

A type of script and address that allows transfer of bitcoins to arbitrary complex scripts using a compact hash of that script.

This results in much smaller transaction fees and less wait for the non-standard transaction to get into the blockchain. The actual script matching the hash must be provided by the payee when redeeming the funds.

P2SH addresses are encoded in Base58Check as are regular public keys and begin with the number "3".

Peer-to-Peer, P2P

This is a concept that is central to cryptocurrency.

A system of sharing information between individuals on a network rather than going through a central authority.

In the case of Bitcoin, the network is built in such a way that each user is broadcasting the transactions to other users. No bank is required as a third party.

Private Key

A secret piece of data that proves one's right to spend bitcoins from a specific wallet through a cryptographic signature. It is a 256-bit number used in ECDSA algorithm to create transaction signatures to prove ownership of bitcoins.

An alphanumeric string kept secret by the user and designed to sign a digital communication when hashed with a public key. In the case of Bitcoin, this string is a private key designed to work with a public key. The public key is a Bitcoin address.

This unique identifier code is used as a digital signature during transactions. Compared to public keys, which are openly listed in directories of many cryptocurrency exchanges, private keys are intended to remain closely guarded. A private key is used to "sign" an approval of a transaction.

Private keys are stored within wallet applications and are usually encrypted with a pass phrase. Private keys can be completely random or generated from a single secret number

In the case of Bitcoin, a Bitcoin wallet and its private key(s) are linked by mathematics. When one's Bitcoin software signs a transaction with the appropriate private key, the entire network can see that the signature matches the bitcoins being spent. However, there is no way for others to guess a private key.

To maintain integrity and to protect against theft, a private key should never been revealed to others and should be treated as one's credit card or Social Security numbers.

Pool

A collection of mining clients which collectively mine a block and then split the reward between them. Mining pools are a useful means to increase the probability of successful mining a block as difficulty rises.

As the amount of computing power needed to mine a block has risen, those who do not have the resources or skills needed to compete can merge their computing power with others and get a proportional return on blocks discovered.

The rise in pools has also given rise to concentrations of hashing power, leading to concerns of a **51% attack**. So far, in practice, miners have been careful not too violate this limit to protect the integrity of the system and to maintain the value of their holdings.

Priority

A scoring mechanism to help ensure that expensive data storage is not consumed by lower quality and spam. Low priority transactions will not be included by a miner if the limited space is already filled by higher priority transactions. A transaction fee will affect priority.

Proof-of-Stake

An alternative to **proof-of-work**, in which one's existing stake in a currency or the amount of currency held, is used to calculate the amount of currency one can mine.

Rewards for this type of mining are based upon the amounts one has already invested in the particular cryptocurrency in question.

Proof-of-stake mining is generally not a stand alone mining method but is used by some cryptocurrency issuers in combination with proof-of-work mining. Peercoin and Novacoin are two major cryptocurrencies that use this combination of mining method.

Proof-of-Work

A system that ties mining capability to computational power. Blocks must be hashed, which is in itself an easy computational process, but an additional variable is added to the hashing process to make it more difficult. When a block is successfully hashed, the hashing must have taken some time and computational effort. Thus, a hashed block is considered proof-of-work.

Proof-of-work is a result that can only be obtained through the use of computational resources. Hashes are cryptographic problems that must be solved in order for a block to be won. Since it is difficult to solve a hash, the solution is proof that a miner put in the effort to get that block. Changing the data in a proof-of-work requires redoing the work.

The rewards for this type of mining are that one receives coins and transaction fee rewards in direct correlation to the actual mining work one does. Therefore, the more mining one does, the greater the rewards.

Public Key

An alphanumeric string which is publicly known, and which is hashed with another privately held string to sign a digital communication. In the case of Bitcoin, the public key is a Bitcoin address.

A long string of letters and numbers which marks a location on the blockchain where bitcoins can be stored. The public key, or its **QR code**, can be freely shared.

QR Code

A type of barcode formatted to contain more complex information such as addresses, websites, promotions, etc. Since these are easily usable with most smartphones and computers, many Bitcoin applications will show or print both public and private keys as QR codes.

Reference Implementation

BitcoinQT (or bitcoind) is the most used full node implementation. As such it is considered a reference for other implementations. If an alternative implementation is not compatible with BitcoinQT it may be forked. That is, it will not see the main chain as the rest of the network running BitcoinQT.

Reorganize, Reorganization, Re-org

An event where a one chain becomes longer than the one currently being worked on. All of the blocks in the old chain that are not in the new one become **orphan blocks** and their generations are invalid. Transactions that use the newly-invalid generated coins also become invalid. However, this is only possible in large chain splits because generations cannot be spent for 100 blocks.

Usually, newly received blocks are extending the existing main chain. Occasionally, a couple of blocks of the same height are produced almost simultaneously and for a short time some nodes may see one block as a tip of the main chain which will eventually be replaced by a more difficult block(s).

Each transaction in the orphaned blocks either become invalid (if already included in the main chain block) or becomes unconfirmed and moves to the **mempool**.

The number of confirmations for transactions may change after a re-org, and transactions that are not in the new chain will become "0/unconfirmed" again. If a transaction in the old chain conflicts with one in the new chain (as a result of double-spending), the old chain becomes invalid.

In the case of a major bug or a **51% attack**, reorganization may involve reorganizing more than one block.

Reward

The amount of newly mined bitcoins that a miner may claim in a new block.

The first transaction in the block allows a miner to claim currently allowed reward as well as all transaction fees from all transactions in the block.

Reward is halved every 210,000 blocks, approximately every 4 years. The first halving occurred in December 2012.

For security reasons, rewards cannot be spent before 100 blocks are built on top of the current block.

Ripple

A payment network that can be used to transfer any currency (including ad hoc currencies that have been created by users). The network consists of payment nodes and gateways operated by authorities. Payments are made using a series of IOUs and the network is based on trust relationships.

Satoshi

The smallest unit of Bitcoin is called a Satoshi. (1 Satoshi is 0.00000001 BTC or 1 BTC is equal to 100 million Satoshis).

The first name of the creator of Bitcoin, Satoshi Nakamoto.

Satoshi Nakamoto

The pseudonymous person or group of people who designed and created the original Bitcoin software, currently known as BitcoinQT. There are a multitude of speculations on who and how many people worked on Bitcoin, of which nationality and age, but no one has any evidence to make definitive conclusions.

Nakamoto's involvement in the original Bitcoin software began with the publication of the Bitcoin white paper on a cryptographic forum in late 2008. Nakamoto does not appear to extend past mid-2011 when Nakamoto stopped returning emails.

Scrypt

A proof-of-work process that is claimed to be more efficient on CPUs than ASIC miners, and thus more democratic. Litecoin uses script.

SEPA

The Single European Payments Area. A wire transfer payment integration agreement within the European Union designed to make it easier to transfer Euros between different banks and nations.

SHA-256

The cryptographic function used as the basis for Bitcoin's proof-of-work system.

Signature

A digital digest produced by hashing private and public keys together to prove that a Bitcoin transaction came from a particular address.

A cryptographic signature is a mathematical mechanism that allows someone to prove ownership. Bitcoin uses ECDSA for signing transactions. Every transaction must provide a signature matching a public key defined in the previous transaction. In this way only the true owner of a secret private key associated with a given public key can access the bitcoins.

Silk Road

An underground online marketplace operated on **TOR**, generally used for illicit purchases, often with cryptocurrencies such as Bitcoin. Silk Road was shut down in October 2013 by the FBI. The FBI seized about 160,000 bitcoins making the FBI one of the largest owners of bitcoin.

SPV

Simplified Payment Verification. A feature of the Bitcoin protocol that enables nodes to verify payments without downloading the full blockchain. Instead, only the block headers need to be downloaded. This makes these wallets substantially easier to use.

Every transaction must be present with all its parent and sibling hashes in a **merkle tree** up to the root. SPV client trusts the most difficult chain of block headers and can validate if the transaction indeed belongs to a certain block header.

Since SPV does not validate all transactions, a **51% attack** may not only cause a **double spend** but also make a completely invalid payment with bitcoins created from nowhere, However this kind of attack is very costly and probably to expensive.

Stale

When a Bitcoin block is successfully hashed any other attempt to hash it is futile because it is now "stale". Subsequent attempts would simply be repeating work that has been completed for no reward.

When a block is "discovered" any other miners working on solving the block stop and move on to the next one. The block they were working on now becomes "stale".

The term is also used in mining pools to describe a share of a hashing job that has already been completed.

Subsidy

The block subsidy is the bitcoin reward created for generating a block. The subsidy is halved every four years.

Super Nodes

A participant in a P2P network which connects to as many other nodes as possible.

Taint

An analysis of how closely related two addresses are when they have both held a particular bitcoin.

A way of linking addresses by tracking how bitcoins move between addresses.

A taint analysis can show where stolen bitcoins go and could be used to determine how many steps it took for bitcoins to move from an address known for stolen coins to the current address.

Testnet

An alternative bitcoin blockchain used solely for testing purposes.

Testnet is like **mainnet,** but has a different genesis block. It has been reset several times. The latest testnet is testnet3. Testnet uses slightly different address format to avoid confusion with the main Bitcoin addresses.

Timestamp

UNIX timestamp is a standard representation of time as a number of seconds since January 1, 1970 GMT. Usually stored in a 32-bit signed integer.

Tonal Bitcoin (TBC)

Adaptation of the Bitcoin system to the tonal system. 1 TBC is defined as 1,000 (65,536 decimal) base bitcoin units. It is not widely used. A transaction is a signed section of data that is broadcast to the network and collected into blocks. It references a previous transaction and dedicates a certain number of bitcoins from it to a new public key (Bitcoin address). It is not encrypted. (Nothing in Bitcoin is encrypted.)

TOR

An anonymous routing protocol used to hide one's identity online.

A browser extension that allows people to visit sites not listed on Google and to do so without risking their identity. It was originally created by the U.S. Navy and has since come to be used by journalists, activitists and others who desire to keep their identities and activities private.

TOR became famous as the way to visit Silk Road.

Transaction

A piece of binary data that describes how bitcoins are moved from one owner to another. Transactions are stored in the **blockchain**. Every transaction (except for **coinbase** transactions) has a reference to one or more previous transactions (inputs) and one or more rules on how to spend these bitcoins further (outputs).

Transaction block

A set of transactions that have been broadcast to the Bitcoin network which are then bundled together to create the next block and added to the blockchain.

Transaction fee

Also known as a "miners' fee". A small fee voluntarily imposed on some transactions sent across the Bitcoin network. The transaction fee is awarded to the miner that successfully hashes the block containing the relevant transaction. The fee is used as an incentive to add the Bitcoin transaction to a block. This ensures that miners will continue to be rewarded for their efforts. Transactions sent without fees will generally be confirmed, however it may take more time as transactions with fees are prioritized. Transactions with higher fees take priority over those with lower fees or not fees.

The fee is expressed as the difference between the sum of all input amounts and the sum of all output amounts. Unlike traditional payment systems, miners do not require fees and most miners allow free transactions. All miners are competing for fees and all transactions are competing for a place on the block.

Many transactions are typically processed without a fee. However, where transactions require coins to be drawn from many Bitcoin addresses and therefore have a large data size, a small transaction fee is usually expected.

Transaction input

A part of a transaction that contains a reference to a previous transaction's output and a script that can prove ownership of an output. The script usually contains a signature and is thus called scriptSig.

Inputs spend previous outputs completely. Therefore if one needs to pay only a portion or some previous output, the transaction should include extra change output that sends the remaining portion back to its owner on the same or different address.

Coinbase transactions contain only one input with a zeroed reference to a previous transaction and arbitrary in place of script.

uBTC

A micro bitcoin, or micro. 0.000001 BTC.

Unconfirmed transaction

A transaction that is not included in any block. Also known as a "0-confirmation" transaction.

Unconfirmed transactions are relayed by nodes and stay in their **mempools**. Unconfirmed transactions stay in the pool until the **node** decides how to dispose of it, finds it in the blockchain or includes it in the **blockchain** (if it is a **miner**).

UXTO Set

A collection of Unspent Transaction Outputs. This concept is typically used in discussions on optimizing an ever growing index of transaction outputs that are not yet spent.

The index is important to efficiently validate newly created transactions. Even if the rate of the new transactions remains constant the time required to locate and verify unspent outputs grows.

Vanity Address

It is possible to obtain a Bitcoin address with a desirable pattern, such as a name. These are called "vanity" addresses.

Virgin bitcoin

The reward for generating a block that has not yet been spent, a state which might increase the ability to transact anonymously.

Volatility

The measurement of price movements over time for a traded financial asset, including bitcoins.

Wallet

A method for storing bitcoins for later use.

A wallet holds the private keys associated with Bitcoin addresses. The wallet does not keep the bitcoins, they are recorded in the blockchain. The blockchain is the record of the bitcoin amounts associated with those addresses.

A Bitcoin wallet is a file named wallet.dat and contains keypairs for each address, transactions to/from the address, user preferences, default keys, reserve keys, accounts, a version number, key pool.

The data file for the wallet is wallet.dat and is located in the Bitcoin data directory. It is intended that a wallet be used on only one installation of Bitcoin at a time. Attempting to close a wallet for use on multiple computers will result in "weird behavior". The format of this file is Berkeley DB.

Web wallet

A web service providing wallet functionality: ability to store, send and receive bitcoins. The user has to trust a counter-party to keep the bitcoins secure and be ready to redeem at any time.

It is very easy to build a web wallet, so many are prone to hacks. It is not recommended to store large amounts of bitcoins in a web wallet.

Wire transfer

Electronic transfer of money from one person to another. Commonly used to send and retrieve fiat currency from bitcoin exchanges.

Zerocoin

A protocol designed to make cryptocurrency transactions truly anonymous.

Zero-confirmation transaction, 0-confirmation

A transaction where a merchant provides a product or service before the transmission of the bitcoins has been confirmed by a miner and added to the blockchain. This can carry the risk of **double spending.**

When bitcoins are sent to an address but the transaction is not yet included in a block, it is considered a zero-confirmation transaction. The on-average confirmation time of ten minutes may be too long for many everyday purchases. Therefore some merchants will take funds that have arrived in their wallet as adequate proof that the transaction has taken place and conclude the sale.

This can carry the risk known as a **51% attack** or a **double spend** attack. An attacker can make a payment, wait until the merchant accepts some number of confirmations and provides the product or service. The attacker then starts mining a parallel chain of blocks starting with the **block** preceding the transaction. This parallel **blockchain** then includes another transaction that spends the same bitcoins on some other address. When the parallel chain becomes more difficult, it is considered a main chain by all nodes and the original transaction becomes invalid. Having more than half the total **hashrate** guarantees the possibility to overtake a chain of any length, hence the name of the attack. (Strictly speaking it is "more than 50%, not 51%.)

Furthermore, even 40% of hashrate allows for double spending, but the chances are less than 100% and diminish exponentially with the number of confirmations that the merchant requires.

This attack is considered theoretical as possessing more than 50% of the hashrate might be much more expensive than any gain from a double spend.

Another variant of an attack is to disrupt the network by mining empty blocks, thereby censoring all transactions. An attacked can be mitigated by blacklisting blocks that most "honest" miners consider abnormal. Under normal conditions miners and mining pools do not censor blocks and transactions as this may diminish trust in Bitcoin and thus their investment.

A **51% attack** is also mitigated by using checkpoints that prevent reorganization past the certain block.

#

www.ingramcontent.com/pod-product-compliance
Lightning Source LLC
Chambersburg PA
CBHW030010190526
45157CB00014B/2112